Toolkit #1

Volunteer Handbooks

Why you need them and how to develop them

An exciting strategy for your volunteer development program

Marilyn L. Donnellan, MS

Volunteer Handbooks

One of the Nonprofit Toolkit series:
Tool #1: Volunteer Handbooks
Tool #2: The Top Twenty Sustainability Strategies for Nonprofits
Tool #3: Becoming a Tech-Focused Nonprofit

Published by CreateSpace
©2018, by Marilyn L. Donnellan, Author

All rights reserved. This includes the right to reproduce any portion of this book in any form. The author and publisher specifically disclaim any responsibility for any liability, loss, or risk, personal or otherwise, incurred as a consequence, directly or indirectly, of the use and application of any of the contents of this book. Although every precaution has been taken in the preparation of this book, the publisher and authors assume no responsibility for errors or omissions.

Sections of this toolkit are based on *Nonprofit Management Simplified: Board and Volunteer Development,* ©2017, CharityChannel Press, by Marilyn Donnellan, MS

ISBN 13: 978-1986095556
ISBN 10: 19860955X

Table of Contents

Chapter	Page #
One: Before You Start the Handbook	5
Two: Develop Recruitment Policies & Procedures	21
Three: Develop Training & Orientation Policies & Procedures	27
Four: Develop Recognition Policies & Procedures	30
Five: Develop Dismissal Policies & Procedures	32
Six: Compile the Handbook	36
Seven: Finalize the Handbook	44
Figures	**Page #**
1: Virtual Volunteers	11
2: Core Elements	12
3: Board & Staff Roles & Responsibilities	15
4: Policy Definition	18
5: Sample Board Recruitment Policies & Procedures	22
6: Sample Committee Recruitment Policies & Procedures	23
7: Sample Program Volunteer Recruitment Policies & Procedures	25
8: Sample Orientation & Training Policies & Procedures	29
9: Sample Recognition Policies & Procedures	31
10: Sample Dismissal Policies & Procedures	34
11: Sample Table of Contents for a Handbook	38
12: Sample Welcome Page	40
13: Handbook Formats – Pros & Cons	46

Table of Contents, cont.

Addendums	Page #
A: Volunteer Development Committee Job Description	50
B: Board Member Job Description	52
C: Sample Board Matrix	54
D: Board Member Application	56
E: Commitment to Serve, Confidentiality Form for Board Members	57
F: Board Officer Job Description	59
G: Sample Committee Job Description	61
H: Committee Volunteer Application	63
I: Commitment to Serve, Confidentiality Form for Committee & Program Volunteers	64
J: Sample Orientation & Training Agenda	65
About the Author	**66**
Other Books by Donnellan	**66**
Connect with the Author	**67**

Chapter One

Before you start on the Handbook

You may already be convinced of the need for a volunteer handbook, but before we get to the "how" of putting one together, there are some basic things to consider. First, understand that volunteer handbooks are probably one of the most underutilized but potentially most important tools in any nonprofit's management toolbox.

Overstatement? I don't think so. Over the years I have worked with thousands of volunteers and hundreds of nonprofits. But I can count on one hand the number of good volunteer handbooks I have seen. And, I can only recall a handful of good volunteer development programs.

Why? Maybe it is because most nonprofits are so busy running programs and raising money that volunteers are an afterthought. Even when volunteer involvement is a grant requirement for in-kind contributions or as a part of matching funds, I have heard staff complain that volunteers "just get in the way of me doing my job."

How sad. Volunteers are often the biggest untapped resource for any nonprofit. Volunteerism in the United States of America is unmatched anywhere in the world and is foundational to our history and our character as a nation. Yet it sometimes seems that we leave the development of volunteers in our organizations to chance or as something we will deal with only when we don't have anything else to do.

I am absolutely convinced that regardless of the size, type of nonprofit, or number of volunteers involved in your organization, deciding to put together a volunteer handbook could well revolutionize your nonprofit.

Here are just a few reasons why:
- The process of putting together the handbook will identify gaps in your volunteer development program,
- The handbook will crystalize the critical roles volunteers play in your nonprofit,
- Use of the handbook will expand the role of volunteers in your nonprofit,
- The handbook will increase the number of high capacity volunteers in your nonprofit.

To clarify, high capacity volunteers are volunteers that operate at the fullest extent of their talents and capabilities, enhancing the vision and mission of your nonprofit. When more volunteers become high capacity volunteers, a lot of positive things can occur:

- Individual giving to your nonprofit increases because volunteers always give more,
- Staff are freed up to do the jobs they were trained to do,
- Requirements for in-kind contributions on certain grants are easily met,
- The nonprofit gains new perspectives on how things might be done by listening to volunteers with high levels of knowledge and experience.

Can these positive things occur without putting a handbook together? Absolutely. However, the chances of them occurring on their own diminish since there is often not a motivating factor. A volunteer handbook can be just the ticket to jumpstart or enhance your volunteer development program.

Define the Roles of Volunteers

Before I get into the specifics of developing the handbook, I am going to digress for a moment and quote from my book, *Nonprofit Management Simplified: Board and Volunteer Development*. The book includes a lot of sample policies and procedures on how to set up a volunteer development program and much of the material in this toolkit comes from it. This quote is based on a true story.

The potential volunteer had almost thirty years of experience as a nonprofit executive director (ED) and when she retired she decided to look for volunteer opportunities. Over a period of three years she applied to be a volunteer at several organizations, without success.

One nonprofit ED was overheard telling his vice president that he was "intimidated" by her wealth of experience so he did not want her working as a volunteer at his nonprofit. Another ED appeared eager for the retiree's help, so she completed the application and even went through a criminal background check. She never received a call back after she submitted the application, despite two follow-up calls and even though the background check was spotless.

A third nonprofit asked for her input and help on the development of two major projects. But two years later the ED of the nonprofit had done nothing to implement the projects the retiree had worked on, and never called her to let her know why.

Unfortunately, the retiree's experiences, a true high-capacity volunteer, in trying to volunteer are not unusual because:

- A nonprofit may have no written policies and procedures for the recruitment, training, recognition and dismissal of volunteers.

- They are not serious about wanting high-capacity volunteers like the retiree.
- They have no clue how to incorporate very experienced and talented volunteers into their nonprofit's programs.

How sad the nonprofits in the example and the community lost a high-capacity volunteer because the nonprofits where she applied didn't know how to incorporate her into their programs.

Don't make that same mistake. Use the volunteer handbook as a tool to start or expand your volunteer program. Believe me, you'll be glad you did.

Secondly, let's look at some basics of volunteer development that are fundamental to any volunteer handbook.

Types of Volunteers

There are at least five types of volunteers in any nonprofit. Deciding how your handbook will be set up to address the needs of these types of volunteers is an important first step. Do you want one handbook for all the various types of volunteers, or a separate handbook for each type of volunteer?

The reality is in many nonprofits a volunteer might serve in several volunteer roles: board volunteer, committee volunteer, or program volunteer. Or they might serve as a virtual volunteer offsite or be a volunteer with a disability. Do you want the volunteer to have to review several handbooks, or one? So, let's first define each type of volunteer to help you decide how you should set up your handbook.

Board of Directors: Members of the board (who are volunteers) are usually recruited for their passion or commitment to the mission of the nonprofit, because they represent a specific stakeholder, or because their community leadership or financial contribution can be a source of help to the nonprofit.

The primary roles of a board member are to legally govern the nonprofit through thoughtful and workable policy setting, monitoring policy and program implementation, strategic planning, ED oversight, financial oversight, public relations and fundraising.

Committee Volunteers: Volunteers who act in advisory roles to board level standing committees or task forces usually bring to the committee high degrees of expertise in specific areas. A marketing committee, for example, could be composed of volunteers with marketing and/or media background and experience.

While their recommendations may eventually trigger a board policy, the committee volunteer's primary role is advice. Advisory boards are in the same category as committee volunteers. Board members often sit on committees[i] providing advice to staff.

Program Volunteers: Many volunteers perform duties that might ordinarily be done by staff. Program volunteers serve food at a soup kitchen, baby-sit for young mothers who need some time off, develop and run a fund-raiser, or any of a myriad of other activities on which the nonprofit depends.

The primary role of a program volunteer is to support the programs or administration of the organization. Board members can serve as honorary chairs of fundraising events, for example, help with clients, or in smaller organizations run the event.

Virtual Volunteers: Taking advantage of the internet, many volunteers like to work from home and provide valuable services to the nonprofit. Examples of the types of services virtual volunteers might provide are shown in Fig. 1.

Fig. 1 Types of Virtual Volunteering

Research & Resource Development	Websites & Software	Writing	People Interaction	Administration
Grant Writing	Coding	Editing	Counseling	Data Entry
Fundraising	Writing	Translation	Mentoring	Develop Handbooks
Demographics	Design	Graphics	Tutoring	Accounting
Social Issues	Updates	Proofreading	Moderating	Direct Mail

Volunteers with Disabilities: Volunteers with disabilities make up about 20% of any community's residents. Often these individuals are looking for ways to be involved in the community but may need special accommodation because of their specific disability. Many will fit into the virtual volunteering category because of difficulties with transportation or other issues. However, often their resilience and coping mechanisms make them ideal volunteers. Just be sure you avoid exploitation of them for marketing purposes.

Evaluate how volunteerism fits in your nonprofit

If you are like most nonprofits, you focus most of your energy on two key elements: resource development or fundraising and programs. This makes sense because programs fulfill your mission and fundraising pays for them. But there are four other elements that must be in balance to provide a solid infrastructure for the organization, and one of those is board and volunteer development.

Take a minute to evaluate each of the six core elements of a successful nonprofit in Fig. 2 to see how well you are doing in each. On a scale of 1-5, "5" being "excellent," how well is your nonprofit doing?

If your ratings total 30-35, your nonprofit is in great shape. A score of 20-29 is good, 10-19 is fair, but anything below 20 may be an indication the organization really needs help. As you might expect, most nonprofits score 4 or 5 in programs, but generally 2 or less on each of the other five core elements, and especially when rating whether or not they have a never-ending strategic planning process.

In evaluating your nonprofit with any type of an assessment, it is really about striving to achieve balance in all of the six core elements. An excellent, more detailed assessment that can be done by the board and staff is available in the

Fig. 2: Core Elements of a Successful Nonprofit

Core Elements Rating Chart	Rating: 1-5 "5" = "excellent"
Administration (facilities, equipment, human resources, risk management, legal issues)	
Board and volunteer development	
Marketing (includes publicity and brand identity)	
Community Involvement (the role the nonprofit achieves in the community)	
Programs	
Resource Development (all aspects of fundraising)	
Strategic Planning (a never-ending process of evaluation and goal-setting)	
Total	

"Core Elements Assessment," available in the book on which this toolkit is based. This assessment can be used as part of the simplified strategic planning process.

Even this mini-assessment in Fig. 2 can help you see how board and volunteer development fits in the overall functions of your nonprofit.

Understand the roles and responsibilities of volunteers

I can say unequivocally the number one issue creating problems between staff and volunteers in any nonprofit is a failure to understand the various roles, responsibilities and lines of authority. If there is one requirement I could make in any nonprofit it would be to make training on this issue mandated for all board members and staff, eliminating a lot of misunderstanding, unnecessary staff resignations and volunteer unrest.

Fig. 3: Board & Staff Roles, Responsibilities

Board, Volunteers and Staff
Roles, Responsibilities and Lines of Authority

- Board of Directors (Legal Governance) → Executive Director → Staff
- Committees (Advice) ↔ Staff
- Programs, Events Administration Staff → Board Members, Program Volunteers, Virtual Volunteers, Volunteers with Disabilities

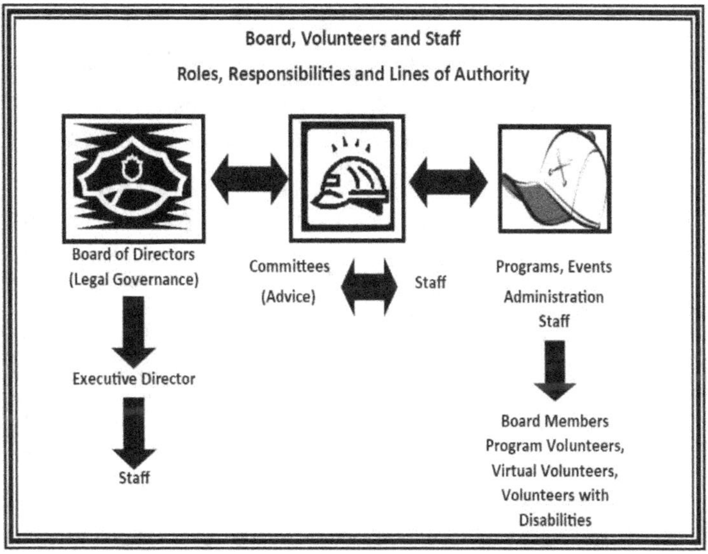

Fig. 3 is a great tool to show the relationships between all three types of volunteers and staff and should be included in the handbook(s) and emphasized in all volunteer trainings.

In the chart, volunteers are identified as wearing three different types of hats. The policeman's hat represents the board member's legal governance role. The only staff person responsible to the volunteer board of directors is the executive director or chief executive officer.

At the committee level, volunteers wear the construction hat. In this role, volunteers provide advice to the staff and staff advise the board members sitting on the committee. There is no line of authority.

In the third volunteer role, program, is where the fun is represented by the baseball hat. In this role board members or other volunteers serve as unpaid staff. Here they are responsible to the staff person in charge of the program or event. When a volunteer is wearing a program hat, the staff person is in authority over the volunteer.

I know of one situation where a staff person was put in charge of a nonprofit's first ever golf tournament. The talented staff person was told one of the board members would serve as honorary chairperson of the event. At the end of the successful golf tournament, the staff person was called into the executive director's office and told she was fired.

When asked why, the ED replied, "Because you didn't follow the board member's orders."

In this case, neither the board member nor the ED understood their various roles, responsibilities and lines of authority. The poor staff person was caught in the middle. She never worked in nonprofits again. What a loss to the sector, just because neither the ED nor board member understood that the staff person was supposed to be in charge, not the board member.

Gather relevant policies and procedures

Now that you understand the basic elements of a good volunteer development program, let's take a few minutes to talk about policies and procedures. Before you start putting together any handbook you need to know what written policies and procedures the organization already has in place for all aspects of volunteer development.

Look in past board minutes for policies the board has approved. Talk to supervisors of volunteers to find out what policies and procedures are being used. Which of these are written down and which are just assumed everyone understands?

The reality is, unless it is written down it isn't a viable policy or procedure since it is subject to the whims of whomever is running the program. Group the policies and procedures by the four categories of volunteer development:

- Recruitment
- Training/orientation
- Recognition
- Dismissal

Try to figure out if there are different policies or procedures for the three different types of volunteers: board, committee and program. Again, group them per the types of volunteers.

A procedure is "how" a policy is carried out. A policy is defined in Fig. 4. In other words, a policy approved by the board does not tell the staff how to do something but only why it is to be done.

For example, if the board has a policy that says a nominating committee will be appointed to bring recommendations for new boards to the board at the annual meeting, it will be up to the nominating committee to decide when to meet and how to vet potential board members (procedures). Simply put, procedures are the mechanics of implementing policies.

Fig. 4 - Policy Defined

Characteristics of a Policy

- **Must be approved by the board, written down and dated.**
- **Provides a framework for staff on "why" something is done not "how" it is to be done.**
- **Can be changed**
- **A broad, governing principle, rather than a program or planning statement.**

Here is where a lot of nonprofits get hung up BEFORE they even get to the mechanics of putting together a volunteer handbook:

Unless policies and procedures for all aspects of volunteer recruitment, training, recogntion and dismissal are developed prior to putting the handbook(s) together, the handbooks will be useless.

And that is why many nonprofit never get to actually putting the handbook together. They get stuck in developing the policies and procedures.

But I'm going to make it easy for you. In the next four chapters I'm going to include sample policies and procedures that will help you get past that possible roadblock. All you have to do is review these samples, decide if they fit your organization, tweak them to fit your needs, present the policies to the board for approval, present the procedures to the staff for their approval, and voila! You will be ready to start your handbook.

By the way, you can simplifiy this process of policy development if you first establish a volunteer development committee. Allowing a board-level committee to be involved in the development and review of the policies to go to the board takes a tremendous amount of pressure off of staff and creates a higher degree of ownership for the board members involved on the board. A sample job description for the committee is included as Addendum A.

So, to summarize. Before you think about putting together a volunteer handbook:
1. Define the volunteer roles in your nonprofit
2. Evaluate how volunteerism fits in your nonprofit
3. Understand the roles and responsibilities of volunteers
4. Gather relevant policies and procedures
5. Establish a Volunteer Development Committee.

Chapter Two

Develop Recruitment Policies and Procedures

The policies and procedures in Fig. 5 are just a few samples of recruitment strategies for board members which could be included in a handbook. Policies are indicated first, with tools and implementation procedures following. A review and rewrite of these recruitment policies and procedures can be done in one hour.

Re-write the policies to fit the needs of your nonprofit and present them to the volunteer development committee for input. The committee will then forward the final policies to the board for approval.

Tools and implementation procedures can be finalized by staff later as part of the development of their work plans. More detailed policies and procedures are included in the book.

See how simple these policies and procedures are? It doesn't have to be complicated. In fact, the simpler the better, especially if you are going to include them in the handbook. By putting them in a table format like Fig. 5, the policies are easy to read and understand.

Fig. 5 – Recruitment Policies & Procedures for Board Members

Policy	Tool	Procedure
A nominating committee will be appointed by the board and will bring recommendations to the board at the meeting prior to the annual meeting, per the bylaws	Addendum A Addendum B	Monthly or quarterly meetings to review applications, term expirations of current board members, demographics and ethnic needs for diversity
The nominating committee will work closely with the volunteer development committee to ensure consistency in implementation of policies and procedures	Addendum F	Meetings will be held between the nominating committee and volunteer development chairs to coordinate efforts
A board member job description and application will be given to all prospective board members	Addendum C Addendum D	Completed applications submitted to nominating committee

The tools should be included in the handbook. And, if the handbook is on-line, items like the application (Addendum D) and the Commitment to Serve (Addendum E) can be hyperlinked so the board member can go directly to the form, download it, complete it, and submit it.

The matrix in Addendum C is a simple way to keep track of board member terms of office, ethnicity, geographic and demographic representation on the board. Including a matrix like this in a handbook is also helpful information for board and committee volunteers.

Fig. 6: Recruitment Policies & Procedures for Committee Volunteers

Policy	Tool	Procedure
The chair and vice chair of all board appointed committees will be board members, appointed at the first board meeting of the fiscal year, per the bylaws	Board committee job descriptions Addendum G	All committee chairs, vice chairs and members will receive copies of their job descriptions
All board members will sit on at least one board-standing committee	Addendum G	At the first board meeting of the fiscal year, board members will select the committee on which they will serve

Let's compare board recruitment policies and procedures to a table showing committee policies and procedures in Fig. 6

Also notice that the application (Addendum H) and commitment to serve (Addendum I) forms are the same for program and committee volunteers. That is because they are not in a legal governance positions like board volunteers.

You may decide you want to add to or subtract from these policies, but at least this will give you somewhere to start.

Now let's look at recruitment policies and procedures for program volunteers in Fig. 7. See if you can catch the key differences between committee and program volunteers. Here is a hint. Program volunteers often work directly with clients. How would that make a difference in how they are recruited and supervised?

Are you sure you have included adequate policies and procedures for volunteers working directly with vulnerable clients to prevent potential abuse or to avoid putting the nonprofit at risk? Does this question raise any red flags for recruitment of board members or committee members? If it does, should you add any other policies to your recruitment policies?

For example, will board members have any interaction with clients? If so, maybe they will need to have criminal background checks, just like a program volunteer would.

Hopefully, by the time you complete this process of gathering, evaluating and developing policies and procedures for board, committee and program volunteers you now have a better idea of how important this step is BEFORE you start development of your volunteer handbook.

Fig. 7: Program Volunteer Recruitment Policies and Procedures

Policy	Tool	Procedure
Program volunteers will complete a volunteer application and commitment to serve form and receive a job description when appropriate	Application (Addendum H) Commitment to Serve (Addendum I)	Recruit volunteers and given them job descriptions and applications. Note: not all volunteer positions will require a job description
Criminal background checks will be conducted on any program volunteer who will have contact with vulnerable clients (children, youth, disabled or elderly)	Criminal background form provided by the city, county or state	Submit criminal background check form Advise volunteer when results are received Volunteer will not work alone with clients until background check is approved, and then will be partnered with an experienced volunteer for one year.

Importance of a Volunteer Database

I cannot emphasize enough how important an accurate volunteer database is, not only for tracking volunteer hours, terms of service (for board members), but also to use for every aspect of volunteer development.

Good volunteer records are essential. I had one volunteer who had served for more than 40 years, but no one had put in the records that he despised plaques. I made the mistake of giving him a plaque in celebration for his 40 years of service and he was livid. He would rather have had the money for the plaque going to the programs. I learned a lesson from that: be sure the volunteer database includes how the volunteer wants to be recognized.

Chapter Three

Develop Training and Orientation Policies and Procedures

By establishing policies and procedures for the recruitment of all types of volunteers first, it is much simpler to then develop training and orientation policies and procedures. Develop training and orientation strategies that are geared to each type of volunteer. Vary the availability of the training to fit the needs of the volunteers.

As an experienced trainer, my first reaction would be to give you a whole chapter on the mechanics of a good training, but since the purpose of this guide is the development of a volunteer handbook, I will restrain myself and instead focus on sample policies and procedures for the three types of volunteers.

The purpose of volunteer orientations is to inform new board members, officers, committee and program volunteers about the history, structure and mission of the nonprofit, but also to:

1. Orient volunteers to their responsibilities and their relationships to other volunteers,

2. Provide continuity in the information to more effectively fulfill the mission and objectives of the nonprofit.

Orientations of all volunteers might include the following elements:

- History and mission of the nonprofit,
- Organizational structure,
- By-laws, values, policies and procedures (as they relate to the ability of the volunteer to fulfill their responsibilities),
- Organizational objectives,
- Strategic plan,
- Issues impacting the nonprofit and its ability to provide services to members,
- Job descriptions and responsibilities of the volunteer,
- Roles and responsibilities of volunteers (Fig. 3),
- Leadership development (where appropriate or needed),
- External relationships with other nonprofits or organizations
- Policies and procedures related to their area of volunteering.

Because of the critical and legal nature of board governance, refer to the book on board and volunteer development for detailed agendas for board training. Addendum J includes a a sample orientation agenda adaptable to any type of volunteer. Fig. 8 overviews the various kinds of orientations, trainers and timelines for each type of volunteer. Remember, these are simply examples of policies and procedures.

Draft your own, based on what works for your organization. One size doesn't necessarily fit all. There are too many variables, with differences between missions, sizes and types of nonprofits for one orientation or training to ever fit every nonprofit.

Fig. 8: Orientation & Training Policies & Procedures

Description	Board Members	Committee Volunteers	Program Volunteers
Policy	Every board member will receive training within six months of being elected to the board	Committee volunteers will be oriented to the purpose and responsibilities within the first month of each fiscal year	Program volunteers will receive training from their supervisor before starting to volunteer
Type of Orientation or Training	Two-hour board training, mini-trainings at board meetings or one-on-one orientation	Meeting effectiveness, committee responsibilities, overview of the nonprofit; chairs will receive training on how to chair a meeting	Specific tasks, overview of nonprofit, abuse prevention

Chapter Four

Develop Recognition Policies and Procedures

Most state laws define volunteers as individuals receiving $500 or less per year in any type of remuneration (including recognition awards), except for reimbursement of expenses. Make sure when you develop your recognition policies and procedures in such a way as to not exceed your state's financial requirements of volunteer remuneration.

We sometimes think recognition strategies for volunteers will cost a lot of money out of our already lean budgets. Not necessarily true.

At one of my nonprofits, we had the children write thank you notes to our donors and draw a picture with it. We framed their art work in inexpensive frames and presented it to the donors at the annual meeting. Years later I would go into the offices of some our major donors and still see those framed pieces of art hanging on their wall. They obviously found this type of recognition more valuable than a formal plaque.

Although I'm tempted to spend some talking about all the potential strategies for recognition and the hazards associated with them, look at the book for more suggestions.

Fig. 9 focuses on broad sample policies and procedures for the three types of volunteers, just to get you thinking about it.

Fig. 9: Recognition Policies and Procedures

Administration	Board Volunteers	Committee Volunteers	Program Volunteers
Volunteer database will be confidential; accessible only by the ED and volunteer development coordinator	Recognition is the responsibility of the Volunteer Development Committee	Recognition is the responsibility of the committee chair	Recognition is the responsibility of the volunteer supervisor
Funding for recognition will be included in each department's annual budget	Recognition will occur at election and completion of term, and acceptance of an officer position	Recognition will occur at the end of term of service or upon completion of any special accomplishments	Recognition will occur at one-year intervals or at completion of service
Types of recognition	Gifts, plaques, letters, lapel pins	Gifts Plaques, letters	Gifts, Plaques, Letters, Lapel pins based on number of years of service.

Chapter Five

Develop Dismissal Policies and Procedures

Contrary to popular belief, it is possible to fire volunteers, although it must certainly be done with very careful and thoughtful consideration. Unfortunately, too many nonprofits are terrified of firing a volunteer, especially a board member, because they do not want to deal with the potential ramifications. And, let's be honest, few of us enjoy conflict and will do just about anything to avoid it.

But, just like anything, the proper development of policies and procedures will go a long way toward negating problems. Let me illustrate why such policies and procedures related to volunteer dismissals are essential.

At my third nonprofit, I was wined and dined by a local real estate mogul when I first arrived in the community as the new CEO. He introduced me to the mayor and several other big shots in the community.

I was grateful and when he suggested one day that he would be interested on serving on our board of directors, I gave his name to the nominating committee. I noticed a couple of the members looked askance at each other, but they never brought up any reasons why he shouldn't be a board member.

He was duly appointed to the board. The day after his appointment, he walked into my office, sat down in a chair in front of my desk, put his feet up on the desk, and said, "Marilyn, I have been responsible for getting the executive directors of two nonprofits in this community fired, and you are next." He then stood up and walked out the door.

As you might expect, my chin hit the floor in shock. He gave no reason for his statement. When I told the board chair, he blew it off. I also mentioned the situation to a trusted board member who promised he'd keep an eye on him. Within a month he was caught in a flagrant lie in a meeting and the board voted him off the board. I tell this true story for a couple of reasons:

1. It illustrates how critical it is the nominating committee have confidential, open and honest discussion about potential board members. It turned out that members of the committee knew about his reputation but hadn't been willing to say anything in the meeting.
2. There must be policies in place to deal with disruptive volunteers so that staff doesn't end up having to bear the brunt of such bad behavior as I was.

Obviously if there is illegal activity, dismissal policies must involve legal authorities, but too often nonprofits are willing to put up with bad behavior from volunteers and end up losing other volunteers and even staff because they refuse to deal with it. Unfortunately, board members would often rather fire the executive director than a fellow board member.

Fig. 10 is a broad sample policy and procedure for volunteer dismissals. By the way, don't forget to also have in place risk management policies and procedures, including crisis communication strategies to deal with the media when something bad happens. If you don't control the message, the media will.

Fig. 10: Sample Dismissal Policy

Reason for the Dismissal Policy:
We believe that if there has been proper recruitment and training of volunteers, there should be no need to dismiss a volunteer for any reason. However, situations may arise where volunteers are just not a good fit to a position, or there is illegal activity, such as harassment or abuse. All volunteers serving in positions with job descriptions will be asked to sign a "Commitment to Serve" that includes an overview of their responsibilities and an agreement that will adhere to the following dismissal policies and procedures. Every effort will be made to keep any dismissals as confidential as possible, unless there is illegal activity. The nonprofit reserves the right to dismiss volunteers and will use the following procedures:

Illegal Activity or Improper Conduct by a Volunteer:
If a volunteer is accused of illegal activity the proper legal authorities will be contacted immediately and the volunteer will be placed on indefinite suspension from their volunteer position(s) until the charges are proven false. If the volunteer is convicted of the charges, the volunteer will be permanently suspended from holding a volunteer position within the nonprofit. The nonprofit's crisis communication plan will be implemented to respond to inquiries by the media.

If a volunteer is accused of improper conduct, the volunteer will meet one-on-one with their staff or volunteer supervisor and with a member of the senior management team. The meeting will be confidential and those in attendance will make every attempt to resolve the situation in a respectful manner. If there is belligerence or unwillingness on the part of the volunteer to amicably resolve the situation, the volunteer will be removed from their position. They will not be given a different volunteer position unless the volunteer is paired with another volunteer for mentoring and training

Improper Fit of the Volunteer with a Specific Position:
All volunteers will be trained in their volunteer activities and be mentored for one year by a designated supervisor or experienced volunteer. If, at any time or for any reason during the one year, the volunteer or their mentor determines that the volunteer position is not a good fit, the volunteer may be dismissed. Every attempt will be made to place the volunteer in another, more appropriate, position.

Chapter Six

Compile the Handbook

Now that we've done a quick review of the needed policies and procedures for recruitment, training/orientation, recognition and dismissal of volunteers, you are now ready to begin the process of developing a volunteer handbook.

Start by asking yourself the following questions:
1. Will there be one handbook or more? (one for each type of volunteer)
2. Will the handbooks be printed or online?
3. How will they be updated?
4. Is there money in the budget for staff time to work on the handbooks, for marketing and any printing?
5. If there isn't, how will the handbooks be funded? Sponsors?
6. How big will the handbooks be?
7. Who needs to have input on the development?
8. Who needs to approve them?
9. What needs to be included?
10. What will be the order of the items?

11. How will you avoid the handbooks being boring?
12. How will you get the volunteers and staff to read and use them?

To help you answer these questions, I will now take you through a step by step look at a sample handbook, based on a hypothetical Child Abuse Prevention Center. The first page will be the cover, but you probably won't design the cover until after the contents of the handbook are completed, so let's leave that to your design professional.

Caution: Edit all information down to the bare necessity. In other words, don't make the handbook the size of a novel. Keep everything as short and to the point as possible. My journalism professor used to say, "If you cannot say in the first paragraph what the entire story is about, it's too long."

Cut, cut, and cut some more until only the basic information is included. Write as though it will be read by a twelve-year-old, rather than by a college professor. Use color, graphics and lots of white space to make pages appealing to the reader.

Table of Contents

Regardless of the format you use for the handbook – printed or online – you need a table of contents (Fig.11), so readers can easily find sections they need. One of the biggest advantages of an online versions is the ability to use hyperlinks so readers can click on them to go immediately to the sections they are looking for.

Fig. 11: Sample Handbook Table of Contents

Description	Page #
Welcome	1
About the Child Abuse Prevention Center: • Vision, Mission, Slogan • History • Outcomes	2
Volunteer recruitment policies, procedures and documents	3
Volunteer orientation and training policies, procedures and documents	6
Volunteer recognition policies, procedures, timelines, and documents	8
Volunteer supervision, performance reviews, dismissal policies, procedures and documents	`11
Legal Issues: • Health and safety policies and procedures • Cybersecurity policies and procedures • Client abuse and sexual harassment policies and procedures • Disaster readiness plan • Reporting forms for abuse and harassment • Reporting forms for injuries	14
Directory of staff and board members	17
Map of facility	19
Timesheet	20

Depending on how sophisticated you want your handbook to be, and how knowledgeable the person is who is putting it together, you can include an index, too. If the handbook is online, they should be able to do a word search with the "find" key as well.

The detail of the table of contents will depend greatly on the format of the handbook. If it is on-line, it is easy to hyperlink each of the items listed so all the reader must do is click on the link and they can go directly to the page.

Add a Welcome

The first page after the table of contents should be a welcome, like Fig. 12. This is usually written by the executive director and the board president or chairperson. It is a good place to include the logo of the nonprofit, too.

Be sure to change it when needed. Nothing screams "outdated" to a volunteer more than to see a name on the welcome page of someone who hasn't been in the position for several years.

Depending on how frequently the handbook is updated and the format, this page may need to be changed frequently if the board president or chairperson changes every year.

Fig. 12: Sample Welcome Page

We are delighted you have chosen Community Child Abuse Prevention Center as your place for community impact as a volunteer. You are now part of an exciting vision and mission to build a safe community for all of our children. Whether your volunteer time with us is for a few months or for many years, we hope you will find it personally rewarding and fulfilling. This handbook is meant to be an informative guide to answer most of your questions about what it means to be a volunteer with our nonprofit. Do not hesitate to let us know if there is anything we can do to enhance your volunteer experience.

Susie Smith, Executive Director

Describe the Nonprofit

The "About" section of the handbook is where you can brag, but only a little! Start by stating the vision and mission. Neither of these statements should be more than 25 words long. If they are too long they will be impossible for volunteers and staff to remember. It is during the strategic planning process where these two critical statements describing the nonprofit should be reviewed at least every five years.

The simplified strategic planning process outlined in the *Nonprofit Management Simplified* book includes some suggestions on how to facilitate reviews of the vision and mission statement, so they can be narrowed down to useable statements. If you have a slogan, "All Children Safe," it should be included in this section of the handbook.

A brief history of your nonprofit, and I mean "brief," will provide the volunteers with a good backdrop for what the nonprofit is doing today, as well as educate them on the impact you have had within your community.

Finally, here is where you should include a short description of measurable outcomes of your programs. Do not just include number of people served but impacts.

For example, in a child abuse prevention nonprofit, the outcomes would be the number of children who are no longer in abuse situations but who have been adopted or are in foster care, or whose grade levels in reading have greatly improved since they are no longer abused.

Another way to look at it is not how many hungry people have been fed, but how many hungry people you helped to find jobs. Outcomes are about results, not just numbers.

Obviously, to be able to provide measurable outcomes to donors, volunteers and the community, your nonprofit must be set up to properly research how your programs are impacting lives. The book, *Nonprofit Management Simplified: Programs and Fundraising* includes an important chapter on how to establish outcomes measurements, if you are not doing so already.

Include Policies & Procedures

In chapters two through five I included sample policies and procedures for all four aspects of volunteer development for all three types of volunteers. It is in this section of the handbook that these policies and procedures are added. Look at the table of contents and you will see a suggested order for them, including the forms that are shown in this toolkit as addendums. Additional sample policies and procedures for legal issues (safety, cyber security, etc.) are included in the *Nonprofit Management Simplified* books.

Add Directory, Map and Timesheets

Including a directory of staff and board members will help the volunteer understand who is responsible for what within the organization. Include phone number and/or extensions, e-mails, departments or where they are located within the building, their titles, and emergency contact information when relevant. Larger organizations may find that the addition of an organizational chart and even pictures of staff and board members will also help volunteers understand where they fit in the supervisory chain of command.

A map of the facility, especially for larger facilities, will help volunteers know where things are located. Be sure to post maps around the facility, indicating exits and then conduct regular emergency drills that include volunteers to prepare for disasters.

Finally, include a timesheet for volunteers to use in recording the time they volunteer. Many grants require in-kind matches of volunteer time, so this is a critical component of any volunteer program. It is also extremely helpful to keep track of the hours volunteers are putting into your organization for recognition purposes. This includes all volunteers: board, committee and program. Just be sure you have a method in place to record the volunteers' time and ALWAYS keep the database up to date.

Chapter Seven

Finalize the Handbook

Don't forget before finalizing the handbook to have several people proofread it. I had one of my books proofread 30 times by five different people and I still found errors after it was published. So, the rule of thumb is, "You cannot have too many proofreaders."

Give some thought to who needs to approve the handbook(s) before publication: the executive director, the volunteer development committee, an attorney, all the staff working with volunteers? Who else?

Notice I mentioned an attorney. That might be because you have sections in the handbook that deal with legal issues, such as sexual harassment or client abuse. If those policies have already been reviewed and approved by the nonprofit's attorney, then they should not need to be reviewed again. But if they are new policies, it will probably be worth the expense, just to protect the nonprofit from potential legal action.

If you are fortunate enough to have marketing staff, then they should be involved in the design of the handbook. Not only will their professional input help you to make sure it is pleasing to the eyes, but that it meshes with the overall brand identity of the nonprofit. If you do not have a marketing staff, look for someone within your community who has graphic design and/or marketing experience. If this will be a computerized handbook that will be posted on your website, you will need the help of your web master or someone with website building experience to make sure all the hyperlinks work.

Other issues to consider as you finalize the handbook, include:

- Updates: Be sure you know who will be responsible for updates to the handbook and when.
- Marketing: How will you market the availability of the handbook(s)? How will you use it? Will it be a recruitment tool for volunteers or only use it for current volunteers?
- What is your timeline for publication?
- Format: Probably by this time you have already decided whether you will do one handbook or three (one for each type of volunteer) and maybe even the format you will use. But I'm going to expand on this issue in the next few paragraphs.

Determine Format

There are at least five possible formats for your handbook(s). I think it is much easier to only have one handbook, rather than three, simply because often volunteers are involved in more than one way within the organization. And, it just makes it easier if everything is in one handbook. Possible formats and the pros and cons of each are outlined in Fig.13.

Fig. 13: Handbook Formats

Format	Pro	Con
Booklet	Most common; easy for volunteers to handle; easy reference tool; easy to market	Expensive, especially if doing three; difficult to update; special skills to design; easily destroyed
Notebook	Ideal for board handbooks since board minutes and other supporting documents can be added before each meeting; easy to update; useable repeatedly; relatively inexpensive	Can become bulky; board members often forget to bring them to meetings; takes time to put together and keep updated; not sure if owned by volunteer or nonprofit; not useable by other volunteers
Phone applications	Feasible for younger volunteers and program volunteers; portable; could be easily updated	Not user friendly for older volunteers; expensive and could be

		difficult to set up and update; requires special expertise; won't work on every phone
E-book	Feasible for younger volunteers and program volunteers; portable	Limited graphic capabilities; difficult to set up and update; requires special expertise and e-reader
On-line and computerized	Easy to access; less expensive; easy to design and update; can be incorporated into volunteer training module; no printing costs; hyperlinks	Requires computer access; hard to know if volunteers reviewed it; requires some design and computer and website design skills; cannot be carried around as a reference tool; requires regular updates

Finally, in summary:

1. Be sure volunteer policies and procedures are in place first. Do not try to develop a volunteer handbook without first making sure you have solid, board-approved policies and staff-tested procedures in

place for all aspects of volunteer development: recruitment, training and orientation, recognition and dismissal. And, for all types of volunteers: board, committee, program, virtual and volunteers with disabilities.
2. Verify funding is approved for the project. Be sure you have adequate funding for the project, either in the nonprofit's budget or through sponsorships.
3. Determine the number of handbooks needed. Decide if you want one handbook for all types of volunteers, or one for each. If you are printing the handbook, be sure to accurately determine all costs associated with design and printing.
4. Design the format and pages of handbooks. Pick the format most feasible for your needs. Be sure you have the right people involved in the design of each page, so it is easy to read and keeps the volunteer engaged. If they won't read it, it is of no value.
5. Measure the impact of the handbook on the volunteer development program. Establish a way to measure the impact of the handbook on your volunteer development program, either through

surveys or by tracking on-line access to the handbook, for example.

Addendum A: Volunteer Development Committee Job Description

Title: Volunteer Development Committee
Responsible to: Board of Directors
Purpose of Committee: To assure the fulfillment of the board-approved policies and to advise staff on issues related to the recruitment, recognition, dismissal and training of all volunteers for the fulfillment of the organization's mission and objectives, including committee, program and board volunteers.

Key Responsibilities:
1. Planning: To develop short and long-range goals and action steps related to the recruitment, training, dismissal and recognition of all nonprofit volunteers, including committee, program, board, virtual and volunteers with disabilities
2. Resource and needs assessments: To assess organizational volunteer resources available and needed to fulfill the mission and goals
3. Recruitment: To develop and implement the procedures needed for the recruitment of volunteers who will represent the diversity of the community and who will be effective in the fulfillment of the organization's mission and goals; To serve as the nominating task force if the executive committee so chooses
4. Training: To develop and implement the orientation and training methods needed to prepare all volunteers for their duties and

which will develop leadership within the organization and for the community
5. Recognition: To develop and implement the variety of methods for recognition of staff, volunteers, donors and funded nonprofits or programs and to develop and implement policies and procedures related to fair and equitable treatment of all volunteers
6. Board Communication: To keep the board of directors informed on the implemented strategies, results of volunteer development efforts and any potential policies needed which will allow for efficient and effective volunteer development

Committee Structure: The chairman of the committee shall be a member of the board of directors and shall select, or cause to be selected, a vice chairman. The chairman will also serve as a member of the executive committee and shall keep the board informed on the committee's progress on board-approved goals. Most the committee shall be board members. Sub-committees or short-term task force groups may be formed to complete the committee's objectives.

Time Commitment: At least one meeting per month or as needed to fulfill the committee's goals.

(Note: In smaller communities, the consolidation of the Administration and Volunteer Development Committees is feasible)

Addendum B: Board Member Job Description

Title: Governing Board Job Description
Selected by: Nominated and selected by members of the governing board
Term: *Generally, three, two-year terms, but not to exceed six years total without the board member taking at least one year off the board*
Attendance: A minimum of 50% of the scheduled meetings per year. Unexcused absence from two consecutive meetings constitutes a resignation
Responsibilities: (as stated in the corporate bylaws) "…The affairs of the Corporation shall be managed by its Board of Directors…"

1. Policy – To consider, approve and support management policies that promote and enhance the mission of the organization
2. Public Relations – To report to and represent the organization in a positive manner to the public
3. Fundraising – To support the organization with personal contributions and to actively participate in the raising of funds to support the organization
4. Advisory – To act as an advisor to the staff by serving on at least one board committee
5. Legal – To exercise fiduciary and legal responsibility for the affairs of the corporation
6. Planning – To develop and monitor short and long-term strategic plans that enhance and support the vision and mission of the organization

7. Executive Director Oversight – To recruit, train, supervise and terminate the ED
8. Fiduciary – To assure the nonprofit meets the basic Standards of Accounting for Nonprofits and that the financial policies and procedures are followed by staff; to assure the financial stability of the nonprofit

Commitment:
1. To contribute to discussions at meetings, having read background materials and to contribute individual skills and resources as appropriate
2. To observe parliamentary procedures
3. To avoid intruding into administrative issues that are the responsibility of the staff, except to assure their adherence to policy
4. To avoid conflicts of interest and, if such conflict does arise, to declare the conflict to the board and refrain from voting on relevant items
5. To attend governing board meetings, committee meetings, annual meetings and other events which enhance board skills and knowledge

Expenses: Any expenses associated with attendance at events or meetings are the sole responsibility of the board member

Time Commitment: A minimum of 50% of scheduled meetings, plus the annual meeting and other special events or fundraisers. At a minimum, board membership will require two to four hours per month

Addendum C: Board Matrix

Board Matrix - Individual

This matrix is an example of the needed information for three individual board members in a state association and indicates when board members' terms will expire. In this illustration, board members can serve two three-year terms before they must leave the board.

Board Matrix Individual		
	Carlos Hernadez	**Susie Jones**
City	Austin	Dallas
Year elected To Board	2015	1017
Term	2nd	1st
Ethnicity	Hispanic	African American
Gender	Male	Female
Board Committee	Marketing	Finance

Board Matrix – Full Board

This matrix shows the information for a 25-member board. A nominating committee can look at a chart like this and know immediately that in 2012 in the Central region, for example, the first term of one of two board members will expire and there are two additional slots open in the region.

Board Matrix Full board		
Current # of Board - 24	Term Expires In 2018	Term Expires In 2021
Female : 9	3	6
Male—15	7	8
Hispanic—5	3	2
African American— 7	2	5
Caucasian—10	5	5
Asian—2	1	1

Addendum D: Application for Board Membership

Application for Board Membership—Addendum D

All applications for membership on the board of directors will be assessed for the demographic, ethnic, professional, and management needs of the board. Receipt of a completed application will be regarded by the nonprofit as an expression of interest and NOT an approval by the nonprofit as a board member, or an acceptance by the potential board member as a commitment to serve on the board.

Indicate the status of this applicant:

___Nomination has been discussed with the potential board member and they have indicated ___willingness to serve if elected;

___Potential nominee has received a copy of the job description;

___Potential nominee has served on the board of a nonprofit within the past five years.

Person making nomination: _____

Nominee: _____ Date: _____

Preferred mailing address:_____
_____

E-mail/website: _____

Daytime phone number _____

Age: _____ (optional)

Occupation: _____

Preferred title: _____

Business: _____

Ethnicity: _____(optional)

Addendum E

Board Member Commitment to Serve, Conflict of Interest and Confidentiality Agreement

I do hereby declare and affirm my willingness to assume the responsibilities, as stated in the job description, and to abide by the following guidelines:

Confidentiality: To adhere to the strictest confidentiality related to all client, donor, personnel, or nonprofit information, unless there is illegal activity, and to submit to a criminal background check if needed.

Dismissal: To adhere to the policies related to volunteer dismissal.

Conflict of Interest: No member of the board or executive committee shall knowingly take any action of make any statement intended to influence the conduct of the nonprofit in such a way as to confer any financial or personal benefit on such member or their family, or on any corporation in which they are an employee or have a significant interest as a stockholder, director or officer, with which they may serve as a director or trustee or in a profession capacity.

- In the even there comes before the board or the executive committee a matter for consideration or decision which raises a potential conflict of interest, the member shall disclose the conflict of interest as soon as they become aware of it, and the disclosure shall be recorded in the minutes of the meeting as part of the voting record.

- Any member of the board or the executive committee who is aware of a potential conflict of interest with respect to any matter coming before the board or executive committee shall not vote about the matter, nor will their presence at the meeting (electronic or in person) be counted in determining whether a quorum exists.

These guidelines are not intended to prevent or discourage any member of the board or executive committee from disclosing relevant information with respect to any matter of which they have knowledge, or from answering questions or stating their position with respect to any such matter.

ACKNOWLEDGEMENT

"I, _____, a member of the governing board of

_____ (nonprofit), have read the guidelines above and agree to comply therewith. Further, I understand my continuing obligation of disclosure of potential conflict of interest should circumstances or events so warrant. I understand any expenses associated with attendance at events or meetings are my sole responsibility, unless prior approval has been given in writing by the governing board."

_____

    Signature   Date

Addendum F: Sample Board Officer Job Description

Title: Chair of the Board

Reports to, selected and evaluated by: Board of Directors

Term: One year, with an additional year as Past Chair of the Board, beginning with the election at the annual meeting and ending the next annual meeting.

Attendance Requirements: As a member of the Board of Directors, the Chair adheres to the same attendance requirements as a board member, with additional attendance at the Executive Committee meetings. The Chair also serves as a voting, ex-officio member of all committees and task forces.

Responsibilities:
1. Meeting facilitation - Serves as the facilitator of all board meetings and Executive Committee meetings, with voting privileges only in the event of a tie vote
2. Spokesperson - Along with the ED, serves as the official spokesperson for the organization in all matters
3. Supervisor - Serves as the supervisor of the ED.

(From the bylaws, Article V, Sec. 5: "The Chair of the Board shall be the principal officer of the Corporation. They shall preside at all meetings of the members and of the Board of Directors. They may sign, with the Secretary or any other proper Officer of the Corporation authorized by the Board of Directors, any deeds, mortgages, contracts or other instruments which the Board of Directors has authorized to be executed, except in cases where the signing and execution thereof shall be expressly delegated by the Board of Directors or by these Bylaws or be granted by statute to some other Officer or agent of the Corporation; and, in general, They shall perform all duties incident to the office of Chair of the Board and such other duties as may be prescribed by the Board of Directors from time to time. They shall be voting, ex-officio member of all management divisions and board-appointed committees.")

Commitment:
1. To facilitate all meetings in a neutral manner, encouraging input and participation by everyone in attendance
2. To provide leadership to the organization to assure adherence to the policies, ethics, values, vision and mission of the organization
3. To understand and monitor all legal aspects of the organization
4. To seek ways to promote the organization in the community, in the state and nationally, and to convey to the board local, state and national issues which have the potential to impact the organization
5. To assure appropriate evaluation and recognition of staff and volunteer efforts.

Time Commitment:
In addition to the board member and Executive Committee time commitment, approximately one hour per week for organizational duties and for monitoring staff and volunteer efforts.

Addendum G: Sample Board Committee Job Description

Title: Administration Committee or Internal Operations Committee
Responsible to: Board of Directors
Purpose of Committee: The development of policies and monitoring of year-round internal controls for management excellence, and to provide advice to staff on the implementation of policies
Key Responsibilities:
1. Planning—To develop short and long-range goals and advise the staff on action steps for goal completion
2. Resource and needs Assessments—To assess community, volunteer, staff and internal resources available and needed to support internal operations in the most efficient and effective manner possible
3. Finance—To develop and monitor policies and procedures for internal financial management which conform to Standards of Accounting for Nonprofits, and which meet all governmental regulations and requirements
4. Legal—To develop and monitor policies and procedures for risk management that conform to nonprofit standards and which prevent harm to volunteers, staff and the organization
5. Facilities—To provide for the procurement, upkeep and policies related to the facilities and to assure quality facilities adequate for the completion of the nonprofit's mission
6. Technology/equipment—To evaluate and procure equipment suitable for the efficient and effective fulfillment of the objectives of the organization

7. Human resources—To develop and monitor policies and procedures, related to employment of staff, which conform to all governmental regulations and provide for equitable treatment of employees
8. Risk management – To annually review the insurance needs of the nonprofit and its programs; to develop safety and disaster plans and policies, and to make recommendations to the board for any additions or needed changes
9. Board communications—To keep the board of directors informed on the implemented strategies, results of administrative efforts and any potential policies needed, that will allow for efficient and effective internal management that meets total quality management standards.

Committee Structure:

The chairman of the committee shall be a member of the board of directors and shall select, or cause to be selected, a vice chairman. The chairman and vice-chair shall also serve as members of the executive committee and shall keep the board informed on the committee's oversight of board-approved, committee goals. Most the committee shall be board members. Sub-committees or short-term task force groups may be formed to complete the committee's objectives. The treasurer and assistant treasurer shall be members of the committee.

Time Commitment:

At least one meeting per month, or as needed to fulfill the committee's goals.

(Note: In smaller communities, consolidation of Administration and Board/Volunteer Development Committees is feasible)

Addendum H: Sample Committee & Program Volunteer Application

(For committee and program volunteers)

In order to be considered as volunteer, the *Volunteer Application needs to be completed and submitted to the Volunteer Development Coordinator. The purpose of the application is to match the volunteer with appropriate volunteer opportunities.

Please indicate the current status of this volunteer:
___ Volunteer is already volunteering for the nonprofit as: _____
___ Potential volunteer has received a copy of a job description for (position):

Name: _____ Date: _____

Preferred mailing address: _____

E-mail/website: _____

Daytime phone number _____ Age: _____ (optional)

Occupation: _____

Preferred title: _____

Business: _____ Ethnicity: _____ (optional)

Volunteer Experience: _____

Education, Training, Special Skills: _____

Position for which you want to volunteer: _____

"If accepted as a volunteer, I agree to adhere to all the volunteer policies and procedures, including policies related to dismissal and criminal background checks."
Signature: _____ Date: _____

*Each volunteer will complete and submit a volunteer application to the volunteer development coordinator. The information will be entered into a data base in order to provide the necessary orientation and recognition information. All supervisors (staff and volunteer) will keep good records on who volunteers to do what. Such records will be kept confidential. Only the supervisor, governing board and person entering the data will have access to it.

Addendum I: Sample Commitment to Serve

"I do hereby declare and affirm my willingness to assume the responsibilities, as stated in the job description, and to abide by the following guidelines:"

Confidentiality: To adhere to the strictest confidentiality related to any and all client or nonprofit information, unless there is illegal activity, and to submit to a criminal background check if needed;

Dismissal: To adhere to the policies related to volunteer dismissal;

Conflict of Interest: No member of the committee shall knowingly take any action or make any statement intended to influence the conduct of the nonprofit in such a way as to confer any financial or personal benefit on such member or his/her family, or on any corporation in which he is an employee or has a significant interest as stockholder, director or officer, with which he may serve as a director or trustee or in a professional capacity;

- In the event that there comes before the committee a matter for consideration or decision that raises a potential conflict of interest for any member of the committee, the member shall disclose the conflict of interest as soon as he becomes aware of it, and the disclosure shall be recorded in the minutes of the meeting as part of the voting record;
- Any member of the committee who is aware of a potential conflict of interest with respect to any matter coming before the committee shall not vote in connection with the matter nor will his/her presence at the meeting (electronic or in person) be counted in determining whether a quorum exists.

These guidelines are not intended to prevent or discourage any member of the committee from disclosing relevant information with respect to any matter to which he has knowledge or from answering questions or stating his/her position with respect to any such matter.

ACKNOWLEDGMENT

"I, _____, a member of the _____ (committee), have read the guidelines with respect to potential conflicts of interest and the commitment to serve and agree to comply therewith. Further, I understand my continuing obligation of disclosure of potential conflict of interest should circumstances or events so warrant. I understand that any expenses associated with attendance at events or meetings are my sole responsibility, unless prior approval has been given by the governing board."

(signature)   *(date)*

Addendum J: Board & Volunteer Orientation Agendas

Expectations/ Agenda Review

Part I: Nonprofit History, Vision, Mission
    A. Types of Volunteers
    B. History of the Nonprofit
    C. Vision/mission
    D. Outcomes measurements

Part II: Roles & Responsibilities of Board, Staff, Volunteers
    A. Types of Boards
    B. Stages of Board Development
    C. Roles & Responsibilities and lines of authority
    D. Importance of Boards
    E. Legal
    F. Policy Setting
    G. Financial Oversight
    H. Planning
    I. Oversight
    J. Fund-raising
    K. Public Relations

Part II: Board and Committee Structures
    A. Core elements of a successful nonprofit
    B. Committee Structure
    C. Effective Meetings
    D. Conflict Resolution
    E. Volunteer Recruitment, Training, Recognition and Dismissal
    F. Volunteer Handbooks

About the Author

Marilyn L. Donnellan, MS, has more than 35 years' experience as a non-profit CEO and consultant. The non-profits where she served ranged in size from a single staff organization with a budget of $150,000 to a $6 million non-profit with 300 staff. She is the author of numerous articles in nonprofit trade journals and her books on nonprofit management are in use in more than a dozen countries. She has a B.A. degree in Human Resources Management from George Fox University and an M.S. degree in Administration from Atlantic Coast Theological Seminary.

Other Books by Donnellan

The Complete Guide to Church Management (English), Xulon Press,
www.amazon/author/mldonnellan
The Complete Guide to Church Management (Chichewa), *www.mldonnellan.com*

Nonprofit Management Simplified: Internal Operations, ©2017, CharityChannel Press,
www.amazon.com/author/mldonnellan
Nonprofit Management Simplified: Board and Volunteer Development, ©2017, CharityChannel Press, *www.amazon.com/author/mldonnellan*
Nonprofit Management Simplified: Programs and Fundraising, ©2017, CharityChannel Press,
www.amazon.com/author/mldonnellan

Two Faces of Me,
www.amazon.com/author/mldonnellan

Give 'til it Hurts (fiction)
http://smashwords.com/books/view/772465

Connect with the Author

mldonnellanauthor@gmail.com
www.mldonnellan.com

www.ingramcontent.com/pod-product-compliance
Lightning Source LLC
Chambersburg PA
CBHW030047230526
45471CB00003B/979